PINION
an elegy

CLAUDIA EMERSON

Louisiana State University Press
baton rouge 2002

Designer: Barbara Neely Bourgoyne
Typeface: Sabon
Printer and binder: Thomson-Shore, Inc.

Library of Congress Cataloging-in-Publication Data
Emerson, Claudia, 1957–
    Pinion : an elegy / Claudia Emerson.
       p. cm. — (Southern messenger poets)
    ISBN 0-8071-2765-5 (alk. paper) — ISBN 0-8071-2766-3 (pbk. : alk. paper)
       I. Title. II. Series.

    PS3605.M47 P56 2002
    811'.6—dc21   2001038988

I gratefully acknowledge the editors of the following publications, in which some of the poems herein first appeared, sometimes in slightly different form: *Crazyhorse:* "Bone," "The Boundaries of Her Voice," "Her Heart's Cream," "In Order" (as "The Pit"), "The Proof-Meter"; *Louisville Review:* "Ringing the Bell," "Stillbirth"; *New England Review:* "Pinion," "Preacher's Rapture," "What Waits for You"; *Poetry:* "Flood," "The Way to Water"; *Shenandoah:* "The Admirer"; *64:* "Bathing Mother," "The Devil Beats His Wife," "Fine As Silk," "Glove"; *Southern Review:* "Curing Time."

I also acknowledge with gratitude the support of the National Endowment for the Arts, Mary Washington College, and Chatham Hall—and offer thanks to my colleagues Marie McAllister, Gardner Campbell, Bill Kemp, and Mary Rigsby, as well as to Lynn Ackerman and Linda LaFave for reading. Special thanks go to friend and mentor Betty Adcock, who loaned me her sharp eye and advice.

NATIONAL
ENDOWMENT
FOR THE ARTS
Publication of this book has been supported by a grant from the National Endowment for the Arts in Washington, D.C., a federal agency.

Southern
Messenger
Poets

DAVE SMITH, EDITOR

It is better to go to the house of mourning
than to go to the house of feasting;
for this is the end of all men,
and the living will lay it to heart.
—Ecclesiastes, or The Preacher

Still, there will be a connection with the long past—a reference
to forgotten events and personages, and to manners, feelings,
and opinions, almost or wholly obsolete—which, if adequately
translated to the reader, would serve to illustrate how much of
old material goes to make up the freshest novelty of human life.
—Nathaniel Hawthorne, *The House of the Seven Gables*

Let us pause in life's pleasures to count its many tears
While we all sup sorrow with the poor.
There's a song that will linger forever in our ears.
Oh! Hard times, come again no more.
—Stephen Foster, "Hard Times"

*For my family
and
for Kent
with love*

CONTENTS

In the dream that recurs, like a bird returning, the place is still as it was—as though they went away, years ago, fully intending to be back by first dark. Sometimes I find myself at the mouth of the road—the red dust so fine the wind lifts it like a scarf, and I walk down toward the house, past what were the fields of tobacco, the shrunken pasture. One of the curing barns still stands, struggling against poison ivy, saplings, wisteria, but that insistent pull cannot undo the smell of woodsmoke and old heat.

The outbuildings are filled with the rusted detritus of the work: log-chains, slides, plowshares, saws and shears, the harness that galled the mule's rump. Honeysuckle weaves tight through the stalled warp of the hayrake.

The house rises, vacant, the porch and front door lost behind a dense wall of privet I part and pass through. I know I will find my bed still made, and Sister's and my brothers', their portraits staring from gilt-framed soot and glass as though through the fog that is time. There is no one left to know the life that happened here and say their names out loud. I have come home for this.

And then I wake, with their voices turning under my voice, as they broke and turned the earth. My memory of them is this flawed creation; in it, they say what they could not—or would not say to me. I was the change-of-life baby, coming late to them, my sister old enough to be my mother, our brothers' voices heavy as their boots, their backs rigid, closed doors. My birth began our mother's death. Sister raised me, but she raised me to leave. My name—Rose, for the wild, climbing one that thrived outside our mother's window— became a sigh and was for years unspoken. It is as though I was rocked to sleep, to dream over the shoulder that somehow carries me still, weightless as the shadow of a distant bird they could not name from there.

I

PREACHER

The name of the oldest brother, Preacher, reflected only our mother's hope that he might embrace the Word and not become like our father. Preacher's was the last voice of the place, his deafness the wind into which he shouted.

A BIRD IN THE HOUSE

The house wanted me gone, and I cared nothing
for it, living in that one room, that one
season beside the fire I enticed into June,
and I did not know rain anymore, or wind.
Even the front parlor was distant, but I
cared nothing for it, never opened its door.
My brother's room and the baby sister's
were as they left them, as Sister kept them,
and Sister's maiden bed was still made
in the rotting heavens; moths—shy, ravenous—
were let live in the folds of her dresses,
in the rank, corseted air. But I had not seen
her threshold in years. No, I cared nothing
for it, but that was not the same as ignorance,
or memory failing; I knew well what was
combed around me. A generation bore down
to this: a cold kitchen with no woman
in it; her kneading bowl warped in the slow,
idle writhing of neglect; in the flour
wasted were generations of worms gorged
and dead. I dreamed her fists against the rising
flesh of fresh bread; I longed for yeast-perfume.
Every spring, swallows nested in the chimney
of her cookstove, and once a fledgling fell
down. I heard its wild beating behind
the black stove-eyes, a panicked disremembrance
of fire. I lifted it from the cast iron,
and the bird tried to fight new dread from these walls,
shed ashes long cold from its wings before
finding the window open. But I was too old
for omen. There was so little left to know.

ASUNDER

The field before us lay fallow, clover-
bruised and healing, a crop we would plow under.
The plant-bed bandaged what lay just beyond
the willows; I could see it white and clean
through the trees. Mother screamed again,
and I knew by now the women in her room
must be wading in blood. That scream raveled
and lashed Father, whose eyes lay on that fallow
field guiltless as a hawk's, who was himself
so tired evenings he could not speak,
but who climbed those stairs to her, and broke her.

We were all gotten in that raw silence
and came to be with measured vengeance.
I can still see him, resolute, between
the spread legs of a plow, and know how
he looked getting me.
                        But now I was
old enough to have my own son.
                                "You," I did not say,
"you don't remember the time a hen nested
in the dead belly of that apple tree:
a winged tumor Mother said leave be
or I'd lose an eye. I waited till she was
not brooding, and I plumbed what had gone
from rot to hollow, was sunk up to my shoulder
when she bore down on me; I learned the sound
of myself with wings. Mother beat me, too,
the shell breaking, the yolk bleeding from my fist.
I defied her. I stood up and sucked
my thumb; from my second finger, and my third,
sucked what might have left this place, what might
have hatched in the belly of that tree.
On the seat of my pants I wiped a wild
generation.
            'You are your father,' she said,
'you are your father all over again.'"

No. There would be no more voices born
thin as if with mourning.
                              "If you touch her
again, I'll kill you," I said as the midwife leaned
out the window, called down a girl. His shoulders
swayed, gave in.
                         "Don't you even go up
there. You go on up to the barn and sleep.
You can listen to the hogs rut. Maybe
that will soothe you."
                              "Before we were married,"
he answered me, "I used to brush her hair
for her; it was long and cool and deep
and I could not get close enough. Look at you.
You are the measure of it."

CURING TIME

I was all day in a black, ordered heat
so thick and still and sweet I vomited
into tiered darkness. And still the task
fell to me to keep the barn's fires going
all night. If I slept, I dreamed myself swung high,
scorching, strung by my wrists, fists numb.
                                        Awake,
I burned on my cot; I lay there, twisting
tobacco leaves into spirals so tight
they doubled back onto themselves, looped, knotted.
My fists appeared, disappeared, in the rising
light of a wasted moon.
                         Sister's breasts waxed
against it; she was that familiar to me.
There used to be no tide in her. I feared
this changeling who strung bright leaves, her hands
quick and flying. I straddled the beams high
in the swollen gut of the barn, and her laughter
beat past the low rectangle of light—a swallow,
it sought this hollow dusk. Later, straddling
the mule, I knew her laugh in the soundless
distance by her head thrown back, her mouth
filled with sky. She rang the dull bell; it rhymed
itself, calling me to heavy meals,
my tongue dead in my mouth. The water
she hauled boiled against the lip of the dipper.
I could not drink enough. She was fractured
as the moon was by cycles of light.
                              My fists
appeared, disappeared, in rising light
beside a barn that bore in the chinking
the handprints of another generation:
the lone, crooked thumb, here a splay of fingers,
the heel and palm. I turned to wrench the dark,
cured leaves, my hands the hands of a stranger.

WRESTLING BEAR

Lined up with the other rank fools who drank
from a common jar, I, too, guzzled the fine,
streaming bead, and anemic fruit bumped
my teeth as the hawker wiped oatmeal from
its grizzled chin, muzzled its toothless mouth.
He turned up the blunt paws for us to see.
I saw around his neck its claws he wore
strung like awful jewels. I wagered what
I was supposed to: this would be easy
as falling.
    It stood, swayed, magnificent
above us. Still, we laughed, even as the first
man was pried from its insistent, crushing hug.
One by one, men were embraced, heaving
against what was calm—not tame—but careful
and tired—denied passion and passion's long
starving.
    (The story was Grandfather had danced
on the carcass of God and thrown the gall to the hogs:

> *"See these scars, boy?" He ran his finger down*
> *the long gashes in the door. "Spring blizzard*
> *almost starved us all. It was crazed enough*
> *to try to come into the house, so I shot it,*
> *and it fell like a furied drunk into*
> *this very kitchen. We ate high, I tell you,*
> *heart and tongue, and would sleep hard beneath*
> *that hide. I was deaf at last to painter*
> *screams ringing in the woods. I'd learned what I*
> *was made of. You, boy, have never had*
> *nothing to fear.")*

    It sidled open-armed
toward me as if to absolve me at last,
and I backed out of that place, seeing
that what I could not embrace, I could not
let embrace me. The wagers, small, were all lost.

FOR SISTER

I caressed my name carved in the stock,
sought the rib pairing the barrels and thought
I would swallow that bored lie and be changed.
I would extract my name—tooth and ragged
root—from her mouth. I would leave her mute past
forgetting.
                    But the wound might not be
mortal, I could argue, and death only
revision of this hour. And what if for
all time all I could taste were bluing, gun
metal, grief, the scent of her on my sleeve?

THE BOUNDARIES OF HER VOICE

Only cats were left, but they were everywhere—
for years after Sister fell ill and died—in the listing
cowshed, in the web-strung stalls. Kittens
squirmed in a hen's nest. Half-wild, inbred, skittish.
I could not get my hands on one; they wouldn't
hold my gaze. In the stable, others slept
in cavernous milk cans as if they knew something
about milk in white-foaming streams, about warmth.

Once, she kept a white kitten in the house. She fed
it meat from her plate and bits of buttered bread.
She carried it in her apron pocket, and I
could hear it, cotton-muffled, purring against
her thigh as her floured hands spoke in the air
to Rose playing on the floor, trailing twine
in a narrow band of afternoon light.

How many generations removed that taming?
There was one cat, more distant than the others,
white as memory was gray. I saw it, stark
against the hayloft window, and again
at the spring, drinking itself. Sometimes it hunted
the field's edge, just inside the line. Perhaps it heard
her in some inborn dream that kept it here,
within the boundaries of her voice—for that back
fence was as far as it carried. I know.
I had stood at the edge of that same descent—
deaf to the wind with listening. Why else remain,
when it was so easy to step between
the barbed strands that defined us, and be gone.

THE PROOF-METER

All those years the mule's tail swung a ragged
rhythm I likened to the beat of a lone
black wing, loftless, dogged. He could measure
a row perfect, but he could balk and squat,
too, and smile at me. I wanted a machine—
gleaming and blind—that I could finally ride,
that would not sicken, that would not lift its tail
and shit, that would never founder. The mule,
unharnessed, drowsed in the pasture, lowering
his head to random grazing, lifting it
to watch with disinterest his replacement,
sterile as well, and so no kin. I learned
the gauges—the gas and oil, temperature—
and found the proof-meter that recorded
not miles but time. How did it know there was
no distance here? Only these fields, cedar-
bourne, only this creek, rising and sagging
in its bed. The dusk, half-caste, hung on
as the greased, stubborn piston-beat doused
the locusts. The high-beam cut the falling
weight of that night, and darkness foundered on
its one wing. The mule, proving nothing, swung
his sluggish tail, beat out his one known hour.

PINION

I was dragging up the trunk of a wet
red oak when it hung a stump, and I lost
purchase; the tractor reared and fell
back on me. I was held fast there, pinioned, not
dying, growing numb and light, wait-crazed
and finally calm. The creekbank saved me;
its wet reasoned it would take me back, gave
every time I took a breath. I breathed
down; my chest did not rise; my spine fell
into that wet depression, and a beech
tree wheezed, and the creek strangled itself
on the rocks, and time was severed to bleed
beside me and then clot. Impressed: stone, cartilage,
gristle, bone, muscle, clay. I smelled it;
the woods were ripe with it, and the drone of the locusts
rose, reclaimed my voice, disclaiming me.
A lone crow landed on the tractor tire,
and it turned with him, devolving. He looked
at me and spoke, "Be quick now about it,
before the others hear." And as he spun
slowly, the mud fell from that wheel, meat
from its bone, and the crow growled, his mouth
shut. I saw the paling stalks then; with a dream-eye,
open in that feathered belly, I saw the dead
silk, the sweet milk seep from the abundance
I had thought mine. I watched the wind thresh
the fluming leaves of tobacco, the bright glut
of morning glories. The bottomland bore
old freshet scars, and in the woods, fat stumps
oozed my story. And then I was over
a strange country I knew nothing of.
In the meantime a spider had come; from
her distended belly the line raveled,
a fine, umbilical self enjambed, her web
definite in the steering wheel. By a clean
incision, a locust had left itself,
hollow but clinging to my shirt. A kingfisher
had flown down with the dusk to eat where the water

had worried a ragged, blank margin.
Soon they would come find me and interrupt it,
but not before I saw the way things are,
not before I saw, cast from the belly
of that halcyon, its confession
of ribs, a conversion fallen clean and white,
indefinite, on the creekbank's placid sand.

FLOOD

This had happened before: rain that began
as mist—thick and windless, slow to fall.
In the bottomland, bloated spiders
caught fog and bound it; the webs sagged,
white and wet.
            The second day, the creek
argued with the rain, grew bolder before
losing itself, overcoming the banks
that had defined it. Its current cut,
the water grew still, intent on rising.
This changed everything.
              The third day, skeletal
corn-balk was lost. The trees waded in, waist-deep.
Boundaries drowned—the wire dead. I had
moved the cows to higher ground, and, puzzled,
they looked down on that placid other
that was not lake or pond.
             The rain abated
midday, and I knew the next morning
I would see the field reappear as if rising.
I would see the fenceline discovered,
and, more, some ancestral bone, white now
as a root, would appear in the storm-gore
that would gag the creek, sagging in its bed.
I would find crows, those disbelievers, drowned
in their sleep, feathers strewn in the cattails,
their mouths filled with mud.
            But long before
dawn, I would be there as before, at the edge
of what could not be sailed or sounded, watching
moonlight move over the body of that
black depthlessness—and I would be lost
as if I were in some distant place.

THE WAY TO WATER

I hollered. I opened my mouth, and crows
bore in their throats my voice down to the creek-bottom.
The cows would answer—slow, heavy-bellied
echoes; they rose from their knees, lifted
their bodies from the fog. From here, I'd watch
the ascent through the raw defile they had
opened in the woods; above their heads, trees
arched toward each other—edges of a pale
wound seeking to close.
                              Even in dream,
I cut the cord and the belly of the field
spilled from the bale, bloodless:
                              One cow lowered
her head to the hay, and I laid my hand
between the blades of her shoulders. I followed
her down through darkness to water, through what
was healed to a lush, grassy scar. I lifted
my hand from the sway of her spine and slept,
blind, deeper. I was that sure of the way.

HOMECOMING

The door to the parlor was swollen ajar.
Morning glory vines writhed over the threshold,
bearing flowers that pulsed slow and slow, opened
and closed to bruised scrolls. Ash on the hearth
had nothing to do with fire. A snake—cold
black flame—sighed in the chimney.

                                   I climbed
to the second story. Spiders had bound
the tongues of her shoes. Time and wire
had redefined the boundaries of her body;
her best organdy committed to memory
rust and emptiness, *shoulder, breast, hip,*
and *thigh* forgotten.

                          On the roof, the weather vane,
rust-frozen in its socket, argued against
the wind and its quickening rise. The lightning
rods' glass eyes stared down the sky, still made certain
what its cloven tongue did not tell this house.

II

SISTER

This was not her given name; it reflected only the role she was born to. Each time we called her by it, we defined her, until it must have seemed absurd even to her that her name might settle sweet in a lover's mouth, that she might be called by wife or mother. Sister sank into her the way barbed wire sinks into the fleshy waist of a tree until the boundary lay within, fixed as her spine—and as invisible.

Once I found the diary I knew she kept, but it was merely a record of the weather and the work, too much rain or not enough, a calf that died, my birth in the same number of words.

STILLBIRTH

September 1923, overcast

That calf had to be delivered—or lose
the mother, too—its birth, its death. It would
not see itself steaming in the field, or feel
its mother's futile tongue, or stagger
to its feet to get the world under it.
Its memory, first and last, was warmth and water
without light, the measured pulse.
                                          I had watched
the cow grow heavier all summer, the calf
carried in her above the field, knowing
nothing of the field though the grasses
brushed her belly, sighed there; they were
that close.
                    I could close my eyes and open
them again in that watery sway—
all I was supposed to have forgotten.
I could hear beyond the muscled wall
the other's blood and voice, the lungs' relief,
the dead thunder of going to her knees. And always
the ringing bell, constant, as though from some room
above, calling to me. But the wall swaddled
me, doorless, and I, too, backed farther
into the other's body, away from
the hand that would revive and name me—deeper
into the house where no one can stay.

FINE AS SILK

March 1924, warm, fine

The boys would only sop it in their gravy,
talk, if they did talk, with their mouths full
of it. But in the hour the sourdough rose,
I sat in the kitchen doorway and watched the guineas
abandon me to fuss and settle with dusk
in the trees. Mother faint again in the room
above, I listened, heard only the yeast
murmur in its bowl a cold and lazy boil.
I rolled up my sleeves and floured my hands
to punch it down, what was risen pale and full
as her belly swelling even now, the house
heavy with grown men. It would be mine
to raise as they were not, though their mouths
were mine to fill, their beds mine to change,
the red field-mud they tracked into the house,
mine.
    The guineas had hidden their heads beneath
their wings; they blinded themselves as I dusted
the kneading bowl with flour sifted fine as silk, and so
I disappeared as I sank my fists into it.

HER HEART'S CREAM

April 1924, mild, windy

I

How could Mother ever have mistaken it
for the Change. Never mind the eighteen years
beneath which she had lain, a field he had
let go, let grow up in whatever whim
volunteered itself: broomsedge, groundbriars,
saplings in rows grown dull, edgeless. Hoarfrost
turned it, churned up stones. And as a field
goes back to no purpose, she had reclaimed
herself, his hands no more to her than a disheveling
wind that can only go so deep, his desire
no more than a hawk borne on that wind.

                                           She knew,
though, as she knew when she hung the bedsheets
on the line, the wind would seek them out, wallow
in the sluggish damp until they were
dry and quick with it—as she had before
known blood to go to bone inside her, known
two hearts to beat, as she had held another tongue.

II

Every last newborn I had seen come quick
or dead into this world had come finished
in a slick and glistening caul iridescent
as a snail's slow wake but blood-coursed—the kittens
in the pantry's dark, the still fall calf
steaming in the stall. And still I could
not reconcile all that with what now bound
Mother to her bed, her breath rapid
and shallow as the panicked wingbeat of a bird
trapped in a nervous room as it fought against
the wall's stricture, the lie the windows told,
swore to. I thought surely it would escape her,
fly from between her lips like some hard-kept
truth and leave this room, the house, the land,
leave be this woman who gave her daughter
all that rose up sweet in her, her heart's cream.

Every evening, she brushed and braided, telling
how she, too, had been able to sit
on her hair, showing me the thick braid saved
in tissue paper, where it lay coiled
in odd detachment, twin in heft and measure
to mine, where it yet held its oblivious sheen.

THE DEVIL BEATS HIS WIFE

Housekeeping, late May 1924, muggy

The bees, laced thick in the buckeye, went on
with their damp drone; the hummingbirds still nerved
the japonica. Resolved this mist,
like the baby's sleep, could not last, I went
against it, dragged out the parlor rug, as difficult,
heavy, as the body of a grown man.
There was so much to do. I beat the thing
with the handle of a headless axe,
the hickory worn smooth as creekstone, smooth
as silk, and dust rose from the carpet's roses,
raised pink like welts on the backs of my brothers,
dust thick enough, I imagined, for another
genesis, another man to cast
into that ancient sleep; from him I'd steal
a rib and make myself again. Satisfied,
I rested, saw fog hugged the lazy creek
in a daydream of itself, and even
as the sun burned through its back to lull
idle water, the rain came and woke it.

TENT REVIVAL

July 1925, dry

The others my age had grown to women
with their own men, houses, babies conceived
here in last year's field—and here I was
again, hipping Rose. The preacher cajoled
me to be born again. Even in this
heat, I was snow—blinding, deep—fallen pure—
and without sin, without breath. He could spit
in my eyes that I might see, and I would
see men—but they would look like trees, walking.

THE ADMIRER

September 1926, clear

He had before come courting—with pecans
or peaches, berries. I had those times been able
to thank him with one of my pies and be
done with him. For this, though, he would want
supper, to sit at the table with me
after supper. For this, I reckoned he had
spent most of the morning emptying
the sky of its plenty: the doves spilled from
burlap in iridescent disarray,
three dozen at least, a shimmering

bouquet. And so the afternoon was for me
defined; the hour deepened the mound of feathers,
blue-gray, plucked in porch-dusk, and the wind,
disinterested, would once in a while stir them.
I knew they were easy to bring down
over a field where they would fall into
the tangled grasses and go on flying against
what had been wind. Easy—as this was not:
feet, gut, heart, the smooth brow with eyes open
like garnets glowing; I cut and tossed over

and over what was in the end useless
onto the feathers, a last and bloody bed,
or to the cats, who growled and circled me,
to keep the peace. A dove would amount to,
at best, a half-dozen mouthfuls, the dark
breast tender but gristled with shot—black seed.
I threw a whole bird to the nursing cat
and wondered whether the white kitten had opened
its eyes; if they were blue, it would be deaf,
I had been told, and told I could not let it

live. I would see about that. Mother called down,
"How are they coming?" More work than they're worth,
I answered her, for such a little meat.
Even with the birds still baking, yet to be

eaten, with still the biscuits to stir up
and gravy yet to make from the meager fat—
with a strait hour to pass before he would
lean back from the table to pick his teeth and sigh—
I had decided he should have left the doves
their beloved sky, for I would not be won.

BATHING MOTHER

Late May 1927, hot

The cough came and never left, became
a thing unto itself, possessed her throat,
her lungs, the way a whippoorwill consumes
a tree with its convulsive call, willful,
grief-fed. Nothing calmed it, and the season
did not make it any easier:
the fields steamed, tobacco sown in humid
stitches; pollen hung thick as smoke, swollen
on the bees' legs—heavy, sulfur-colored—
as they weaved into the sickroom, and out
again, as though drunk on the fertile world,
its bright contagion.
                Even now, I found
her beautiful, and kept her so, combing
her hair away from her damp brow as the house
below complained, grumbled, an empty belly
I let go without. I sang to her; I read;
I bathed the mother of us all, my hands
dark swallows flying close over the surface
of a pond—whose depths churned, unimaginable—
to make it still, until it was so.

RINGING THE BELL

I

Late August 1927, fine

The clock's coil raveled inside me, losing
time. Noon struck late. But who would realize
the few minutes gained or lost on either
side of it, and what one among them would
ever think it early anyway
or be taken by surprise in the shadows'
slow lean away from the body? Noon was
late, always rude.
                I rang the bell this day
as I did every day to call them up
from the humid field; I sounded the exhausted
hour without passion, the toll measured and calm
as though the zenith opened with no bottom
to come to.
         What I heard was as I thought
the owl far down in its day-sleep, or the fox—
leaving its straitened line in the dust—might hear,
unmoved from its perfect path. What I heard
the milkcow heard, her whereabouts worn
around her neck, a tedious, resounding
jewel, lost drone wandering inside the chambers
of her ear, longing to be apprehended,
understood, an omen. Again, I denied
the sound, reveled instead in the grinding silence
of the clock's tick, the soundless beating of my heart;
I imagined that in time, perhaps this time,
I would pull myself up, return to that flared
mouth, something taken back into itself—some oath,
some prayer, or any word imagined as unsaid.

II

That same late August, midnight

What would the nearest neighbor hear if he heard
at all? The fundamental note unchanged
but the measure I made furious.

30

He would think the house afire, I knew;
he would come expecting the horizon
blood-hot.
                    Mother shone, insensate, the fever
coiled in her; I could hear it hissing.
She had stopped pleading for water, wanted
light, more light, so I turned up the wick to make
the glass go black with that light, and then the fever
closed its candent mouth and lay radiant,
ravishing her cold.
                    The baby screamed;
the brothers and Father sat mute in the kitchen,
may as well have sat on their hands, only
to tell me not to ring the bell, what with
the nearest neighbor a man—and over a mile
away. What could he do? *And if the house were*
burning, what would he do, I answered them,
but watch with us the smoke escape over
the threshold?

                    If death must come, then let him come
riding the hurried chaos of his horse,
the bell's urgent tongue pealing—so that he flails
the animal, begs it to give its heart.
I want him to come as a bridegroom—
made late—would come, frantic in the moon's cold
burn. I want him, as the rope sears open
my palms, to ask me instead to quit and lie
with him—but if he is decided for another,
if this road narrows to her, then let him come quick
and take her now, with my desire still sounding.

MOTHER'S LABOR

Late August 1927, still

You said, *Sister, come rub my back,* and I
could feel it come upon you the way fog
came, froze on the field, the way the womb
abstracted. You recalled the time we had
to help deliver the fall calf, and Father
was shoulder-deep in birth-gore, naming for us
the long spine, the fine rib, the breathless blade
of a shoulder—and what he said, *Ah, yes, this one
will be to keep.*
                              You sank into the bed
where I was gotten, into the story
I had again begged you of my own
quickening—of the time you sang and sang
to make the butter come, and I turned in you
instead—into water long broken, into
yourself. There was no cord to cut, only
my hand to cease making its sense of you.

THRESHOLD

Mother's wake, September 1927, cooler

I washed and dressed you, stroked the smooth inner
cool of your wrist, the place where the pulse had lain,

but you remained formless. The house was filled
with the whispers of neighborwomen, the smell

of cooking. I knew we must feed the mouths
of the living. You had taught me that. Now

I crossed your hands beneath your breasts; you looked
prepared for a journey, preoccupied

with the going. But you would not know anything
of a journey; your eyes were closed against

the way he had cut to this place, the strait
road you once told me you saw as a neat

seam or the familiar scar of a deliberate
cut, the kind a surgeon would make and admire,

pride himself on. No, you would know nothing
of going. And then I saw, instead of a coffin,

a narrow, deeper doorway; in it you posed, still,
completed by the frame, the lintel and sill

of cedar. You balanced on the threshold
of this moment, of the absolute.

I imagined you standing in that entrance,
behind you the house, room after sentient

room, behind you a wake of patient clay
and granite, a shifting shelf of ash and slate—

the biding center of the earth your parlor.
You would not ask me in, though it would be years

before you shut the door and backed into it.

III

PREACHER

Sometimes my brother Nate would look at me from over the rocking of the fiddle bow, from behind some tune, and smile. I don't remember him ever speaking directly to me, and I hear him now only through Preacher's voice. Nate was the one of them who knew he wanted something more. But caught in the current of the work after Father grew too old and then died of it, Nate's desire withered, the way bait sometimes blackened in the traps he set. And when Nate died, long after Sister, he left Preacher nothing even to argue against.

PREACHER'S RAPTURE

My brother Nate was good at what lay flat
for him to stroke, and if he stroked it just so,
it gave the sweetest sound. Yes, he was good
at what possessed a cinched waist, a curly
head, and dark clefts. He said, "Draw a long, tight
bow slow across a tense, tender gut,
and rock it." His pale fingers on that hot,
ebony neck fretted women—taut, full
wet from dancing—drew them to him, their throats
all open. "Dead from the neck up," he'd say.
"When they're through flouncing, I dress them
down and eat them."
                              He did not talk to them
that way. They reeled and quaked and kicked up
sawdust in a cloud thigh-deep. He could have
been a preacher, but a violin cannot
memorize scripture, and he could not call
a name to save him. Nate said all their voices
sounded the same, conspired to one. "The way
whippoorwills have the same voice?" I asked him.
"No. The way a hive of bees hums in the dead
throat of an oak tree, the way I lose myself
in sweet communion."
                              And I was there;
I heard the purl and pitch of that rapture
as if he'd said *This is my body* and was answered
in tongues. And rumors were gotten and borne;
the cleft of the chin, the cast of the eye was
what did not lie. I witnessed he died childless,
and here was his corpse, past discordance, the tension
off, the bridge lost; this was his body, broken;
this was what it meant to keep his silence.

BAITING THE TRAP

This was Nate's lazy living: His guile finer
than theirs, they fell for easy meat in the yawn
of tense, metallic jaws. I walked that line
only once with him; that was enough
to see what struggled in the trap, enough
to watch Nate stand on the pelt to save it
from blemish. I felt that growling through the soles
of my boots. I felt my own bones hum. And for what,
I asked, and he said, "A woman's tired desire
to swaddle herself in something soft and wild."
"Man has no advantage over the beasts," I said;
he wrenched open that jaw, disputed me.
Then he reversed her on a board, and her inner
skin showed white—exposing no secret
after all—already something unto itself,
cleansed against what lay now in the dust and drew
fat, black flies. "For the fate of the sons of men
and the fate of beasts is the same." And he answered,
"This is the only resurrection."
                                        He could not
frighten me then because I believed he was
lost. I waited past the yammering dusk;
I watched his shadow wash up. Around me
heavy sloes hung, clotted. Their bitter
seeds—bones in the womb—I crushed between my teeth.
I watched the wind-flayed willow braid, unbraid,
longing for an admirer, a looking glass.
I ran my tongue in one sweet hull, in the bruised,
immanent void I could not swallow. I
would go in and sit at the supper table
with him, but not before I saw a star
falling burn past its sudden unbecoming—
its fast, evanescent scar—to what stays.

WHAT WAITS FOR YOU

That night fought his dying as I fought him.
By now I could knock the hate back straight,
with no chase of reason. I would not gag
on it any longer; neither would I wish
for something sweeter. I sat on his bed
for those slow-thrashing hours while he pleaded
with me to kill him. I refused, would not
tell him where the shells, unspent, lay heavy
in wait. Instead, I told him a story:

I never knew how you caught it to try
to kill it that way, though I had seen you
catch flies in your fast fist; I had seen you
dismember spiders, fascinated as their legs,
distracted, remembered motion. I watched
you weight the thrush cupped in your hands, sink
it in the rain-barrel, in the deep, false measure
of falling weather, saw the fear rise
in bronze eyes, and the wing-stirred wake claim
flight in the wrong medium, and I turned,
grabbed a tobacco stick, and flayed your cap
from your scalp, your scalp from your bone, aiming
for the coiled quick of you when I failed, plunged
my arms in the water instead and saved
the thrush, hurled it back at the stunned sky,
and the wing-scud marked that bitter rain's
second fall. We were bathed in it.
                                        Did you hear
at dusk the thrush's eloquence unchanged?
Now there was only the wind in the dead,
unshed leaves of the beech tree—a bronze rasp,
and beyond sound, corn-stubble fast in hoarfrost,
and the rows' frozen yawning—the field's rigor.
I prayed that was what waited for you: Your soul
cast into that mottled breast, rain filled
your hollow bones, and you descended a slow,
stale wind—a stone on your foot, until the rain
exhaled you, revised itself—a dead well—
and above you my face, grown still, on the water.

WAKE

I was old but tried walking out, bowed my head
against the wet winding-sheet that shrouded

house and field. That faultless mask froze, bore
my weight the instant before breaking. I broke

it over and over. At last I fell back,
reentered the house to hold a wake

those nights, refused to see him in a dream.
His eyes I left open so I would not believe

him sleeping. I turned the mirror's face
to the wall, fed the fire, and wondered if the swayed

house would bear that weight. Sister's jarred
peaches in their sweetness turned dark

beneath their wax seals—as the pond
beneath its thick margin of ice churned;

soon the wasps would rouse themselves from sleep, wash
their faces. Because he refused to quit this flesh,

thunder shook the house loud enough to wake
the living; the dead were already watching.

Then I believed he would leave me if I
washed him. I reversed his pockets, and fine

pollen was cast to the floor; from his shirt,
slow moths rose. I imagined I hurt

him, heard him rage at my hands on his face,
the warp of the razor sharp and cautious.

He hissed *Come on, do it, do it,* as if
it were not already done. With his knife,

I pared his nails; I washed the soles of his feet
and then I bound him in his feverish sheet.

As if I could sew blind, ripened sloes again
into their hulls. I had not prayed; still, someone

was coming down the road. The crows refused
the sky above the melting field, accusing

me of it. But he had left it to me, always,
to own the cold, closed wings of this house.

THE GATE COMPLAINING

I knew what nothing there was to fear: My heart
stopped would not mean I was gone farther
than that wracked plot of graves. I knew it was Nate,
bored soul, who swung the gate complaining. There
was no grain to cleave. An untended spring
boiled back into itself. My mouth was a well
my face caved into. I had a dream once
of leaving, but in it the road burned. My fists
smoldered. I knew then I slept and would sleep
all my nights in that wet winding-sheet.

IN ORDER

Underneath the packhouse there was
a pit where tobacco leaves, cured
and brittle, were kept in the damp
to make them pliable again.
When I was a boy, I placed
my palms against the smooth, dank walls
that bore no pale root, learning the borders
of the place where the dark was
in order.

        As I descended
again to it, a strand of abandoned
web drifted from the sagged rungs
of the ladder at whose feet
I saw the stray bones of a hound—
drawn to this as to water—dream in
the dust our common restlessness.

CAUL

My hand floated before me, the scored palm
pale, disfamiliar. It beckoned me. Thirst
grew like a gourd, a swollen void. I had
seen the moon fall into a well and float
there, while it hung, umbra and bone, above.
I had placed my lips against my lips
and drunk myself. And still I lay on the water.
I drew up the sheet to cover my face
against the heat. I saw the window as I
first saw it, through a caul, breathless.

HOARFROST

A pale rime survived the night in long cedar-
shadows I broke beneath my feet. The field
had lost its voice; cut, dried, spiraled, and baled,
it saved itself for winter, for this retelling:
I had delivered a dead calf with a rope
and a come-along. I had pulled the headstone
the same way from the suck of its grave.
With my knife I had dug mud from the serifs
of my own name. In those days there were things
worth saving: the womb for the fall calf,
the name a bridegroom would give. So I
worked the wind-tense fields and waited—turned
again and again the mirror's crazed face
to the wall—and still, I would turn under
the hay-balk and open the field for seed.

BONE

It was first dark when the plow turned it up.
Unsown, it came fleshless, mud-ruddled, nothing
but itself, the tendon's bored eye threading
a ponderous needle. And yet the pocked fist
of one end dared what was undone
in the strewing, defied the mouth of the hound
that dropped it.
                    The whippoorwill began
again its dusk-borne mourning. I had never
seen what urgent wing disembodied
the voice, would fail to recognize its broken
shell or shadow or its feathers strewn
before me. As if afraid of forgetting,
it repeated itself, mindlessly certain.
                                    Here.
I threw the bone toward that incessant claiming,
and watched it turned by rote, end over end over end.

IV

SISTER

She never wrote once that she was sick, not in a letter, not in the diary. Perhaps she did not know. It was as though she chose not to get up one morning.

I survive them all, but I find I have become the house they keep. And it is to Sister I owe what she could not herself afford, this room with its fugue of words.

CURING TIME

Stringing—August 1928, hot and humid

My muslin shift clung to me, wet and close
as the mist that had been burned off the creek's back
an hour ago. The ground-pulling was done,
and the heavy dew gone from the leaves yet
to be pulled. The mule plodded up and past me,
stopped where he had stopped before, and would again.
He wore blinders and so would not meet my
eye. Blinded from what, I wondered, the strait
sameness of the field's rows, this easy maze?

If he could see in full that endless grid
he might rouse himself from his standing sleep
to rear frothing against it. His head bowed,
he swung his tail instead, and black flies rose
in an angry sigh from the shimmering
blond mirage of his flesh.
                                    Rose appeared
holding a tobacco worm, bloated-green,
and waited for me to watch while she
pulled off its head—the head of a prophet

hard-sought, hated, but much-heeded. She got
a penny for every one she killed,
and we had yet to see this season what
the thing foretold—itself with wings. It wanted,
I supposed, only what I wanted,
to love this given lot, to take this fickle
plenty as wished for, and live long enough
to crawl wet from the womb that was my body,
claiming the wind above the field as much

as I did claim the field, finding that low,
familiar sky far enough to go.
And all the while my hands flew before me,
could well have been any one woman's
as I strung the leaves, hand after hand,
for the boys to hoist whole acres into

the hot, hermetic night of the curing barn.
Even in a hundred years, when the brighter heavens
would be pulled down inside that one room, when it

would have given way to the slow cajole of poison
ivy, honeysuckle, sumac, when the wind
would enter what had been made tight against it,
this place would yet smell of a heat ordered,
measured to *fix* and *dry* and *scorch;* its breath
would still be mine, its sanctuary ever
night in its former world. The string passed through
my hands, and it was as though a mile lapsed,
then another; the line would not be

measured any other way. All those miles,
raveled, saved like odd buttons, scrap cloth,
soap slivers, pins, that image of myself
in the spooled distance. From there, I might believe
it finished once and for all, the crop made
in spite of the field's griefs: sun, drought, sucker, worm, and mold.
In spite of this, I would see it cured at last,
stripped clean of all the hail had left, naked stalks
strict witness to what I had devoured: all

these hours unmeasured as one. A crow
dropped from the sky to stroll, a frocked preacher
among the damsons, already falling,
and like a preacher panted, lusty here
in the midst of this much loss. The cows
stood marble-like, the color of headstones—
and in their slow schooling crowded the shade to carve
the hard salt-block with stubborn tongues: *To live
in hearts we leave behind is not to die.*

GLOVE

Late August 1928, cloudy

I

All afternoon as I snapped beans, as my lap
filled with the sound of a man's knuckles cracking,
she flew about me. I liked to imagine
it was the same wren, come year after year
to the back porch, who chose to nest here
amidst the mess the boys created. She found
in it a wealth of hollows. One time she chose
a swinging gourd, one year a boot, and though
the boys fussed, I would not allow them to disturb
her. Last year, she finally decided
on a can of rusty nails that had fallen
over, and she built on the frozen spill.

She never chose well, and this was even
more precarious: on the narrow
shelf behind me, a lone work glove—molded
open, like the bronzed cast of a hand—cupped
the emptiness she claimed.

                    Once, in the dusk
of the root cellar, I shuffled heavy jars
of beets, peach halves, snaps, tomatoes. Nothing
looked good in that light. The jars I had yet to fill
lined the bottom shelf, and a shadow in one
drew me down. What drew a mouse into that
empty black mouth? Once there, how long did it pedal
against smooth, invisible walls in full
sight of all it had left behind, of all
it could not reenter? The skeleton reminded
me of a ship in a bottle, sails furled, its ribs
a fragile hull, the skull a socketed prow,
bound to take on nothing as it cut a static sea.

II

At first, the wren stole close by: from the abandoned
web of a spider, from the broom. Then she left
me for lichen, moss, a long, coarse hair

49

from the mule's tail. She worked, ecstatic;
in her mouth, she carried the earth, though she would
lay her eggs where the palm's salty ache had been.

We worked on. Beyond us, a hawk fell
like a blade into the field where the cow
rubbed her broad, whorled forehead against the knot
on a cedar. That shadow the dead persimmon
tree cast on the chimney darkened until
it was again a scar—or, no, the wound
itself—or any fissured reverie
into which I could fall. And when night closed
it, the seam would take me with it.
                                             Sometimes I felt
as though I put up food for a great flood,
that I filled the hull and waited for a certain
rain, or perhaps that flood had long come
and frozen, invisible, the world beyond
sunken, the ghost town with it—and now I
waited, icebound, for the day when the bird
would not return, when she would instead
disinherit the habit of this place.

THE DEER

October 1928, summer-like

I had known the dog before in fall to bring
up a foreleg with its black hoof—delicate,
new, shined as patent leather—or the spine
still wearing its remnant of hide. This day
he came, heavy-footed and gaunt, onto
the porch bearing only the deer's lower
jaw that held still its neat teeth in the V
the body had followed in a bounding
wake. I had known geese to leave in that same
shape, the first bird threading some invisible
needle while below it I let down the hem
of Rose's dresses, severing the thread
with my teeth, or quilted down the sky,
pieces of flight in my lap.
                              The jawbone
lay time-scoured, a clean offering. Detached,
it had been what mine was—the cradle
of the tongue—and its last bed. I knew
then I bore in me the form of this slow
migration, the turn to the tropic of bone.

SNOWBOUND, CHRISTMAS

December 1928, blizzard

The almanac predicted it—and now
at noon the birds retreated as at dusk
into the cedar, though the winter wheat still showed
green beneath the snow—light as a veil
of lace—and the field shone copper with broomsedge.
The road burned red for another hour before the world
revised itself and took back the pond, the fenceline.
Trees kneeled before us while we hauled water
for the animals, then for us, while we brought
in the firewood. The water would freeze
in the bucket before dawn—but for now
the kitchen warmed with the hen baking,
and the cat yawned—her tongue, her throat a glozed
coal—before she curled around herself.
And with no hope of company or kin
we breathed, relieved at a sudden joy.
At last, we could not leave. We brought up
the apples we had stored in the cellar,
popped corn dried in the husks. It exploded
into white over the fire while the cradle
of ice stilled all that lay within it. We
lifted the violin from its case, from
its green velvet sleep, and sang then, our shadows
on the walls where they wrestled, strange, gilded
angels, with the portraits' grave faces—those hated
likenesses: *You—you are so like your father.*
The bow droned. We drank the last of Mother's
wine she had made from sloes grown in the frozen
arbor. The fire died down to the voices
of birds, to ash, then to our own voices
singing out as one from the burning tree.

ON THE DAY WHEN SHE IS SPOKEN FOR

To Rose

Because all it called, finally, was death,
I had torn out its tongue, left the bell empty
as the mouth of the dead, empty as my own mouth.
I rejected its blunt immortality,

refused at last the hard *come up, come, come*
to me it was cast to say, that verse
recited without change since its conceit.
I wanted wasps instead to fill the bell with a wordless

hum, the gall of another generation.
The cow would be released into the silence
of her breathing, her hips tolling nothing
now. She would be lost to roam, satisfy

her hunger for the fertile wild onion. Yet
even as that slow whimsy spoiled the milk
in her, the mother-tongue would not be let
go. Heavy and earthbound, the whippoorwill

took up, instead of the sky, that relentless
call, and though I despised it, I knew I lived
to urge it still to tell to us our place.
Convulsive first as weeping, the narrative

lulled, wove around itself, around your throat
and mine, a spectral cord that bound us fast
to all I had learned by rote and you would say by heart:
We have a little sister and she has

no breasts. What shall we do for our sister
on the day when she is spoken for? If she
is a wall we will build upon her
a battlement of silver; but if she

is a door, we will enclose her with boards
of cedar. I was a wall. Yes, I was
a wall, no door in it. And I was spoken for
long before I was born. Before I was

conceived, this place spoke for me. I covered
your ears with my hands so that you could not hear
it—or me, so that you heard only your
own heart's refrain revised. You were the door

I could unboard, and over the threshold
you entered the wing I dreamed for me,
greater by far than the house, like the swallow's
wing, longer than its sleek and cloven body,

so that you remained all day aloft,
away, far swifter even than the hawk.
Yes, I was the wall you soared; I lost
your shadow from my breast, and still you did not

release the air. You would always delight
me in your distance—your body, your ear
lost to your cursive, to your own delight—
sharp, incisive, something written there—
and though you could not know it, something here.

SISTER'S DREAM OF THE EMPTY WING

Day breaks first in the throats of birds, and I
arise in the dream, in the cried-for solitude.
The threshold opens onto a hallway I have
never seen, and it is so wide and tall
a hawk accepts it as sky and a fawn
lies curled in sleep on the landing. The wing
opens above and before me, room on
empty room—as though on the moving day
I have never known, but all is familiar
as my footfall on the pine floors—tongues dumb
in the grooves, the house settled before me.
One wall hums, the bees immured, and ivy
climbs it, a backward fall of green water
pooling into air. Milkweed drifts up the stairs
bearing its slim, hard seed, sharp as a needle.
I am guest in this indwelling, a clean
counterworld of unscarred floors, shimmering
as though with dew, and the flawless hearth that has
not known fire. Birds nest in the cool chimney,
purr there.
                    These walls, bare of portraits, have not
known the tick of a clock, or the sigh of love,
the breathed relief of afterbirth, the grief,
the sleep that calls us all.
                                        Through room after room
I follow the mockingbird, mocking
no other, calling out with original
voice the generation that speaks also
in me, in this wing that leaves the house
behind it forgotten—where I will
not wake, the cage of my ribs swept clean.